KU-363-695

PICTURE
DICTIONARY

Written by
Evelyn Goldsmith & Amanda Earl

Illustrated by Lyn Mitchell

Produced by Times Four Publishing Ltd

HARRAP

Contents

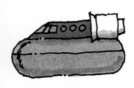

Section 1 **Thematic dictionary**

Introduction	3
Your body	4
Your clothes	6
In the bedroom	8
In the bathroom	10
In the kitchen	12
In the living room	14
Pets	16
Food	18
Play	20
In the garden	22
Minibeasts	24
At school	26
In the park	28
On the building site	30
In the town	32
In the supermarket	34
In the country	36
On the farm	38
Travelling	40
On the beach	42
Camping	44
In the safari park	46
In the amusement park	48
Having a party	50
Underwater	52
Movement	54
Sounds	56
Shapes, colours and opposites	58
Seasons	60
World of stories	62

Section 2 **Alphabetical dictionary**   65

This book was conceived, written, edited and designed by Times Four Publishing Ltd
Art and editorial direction: Tony Potter
Editors: Amanda Earl and Penny Horton

First published in this edition in Great Britain in 1990 by HARRAP BOOKS Ltd, Chelsea House, 26 Market Square, Bromley BR1 1NA

Copyright © 1990 Times Four Publishing Ltd
All rights reserved.
No part of this publication may be reproduced in any form or by any means without the prior permission of Harrap Books Ltd.

ISBN 0 245-60061-2 (Picture Dictionary)

Typeset by JB Type, Hove, E.Sussex.
Colour separation by RCS Graphics Ltd
Printed in Scotland by Cambus Litho, East Kilbride

All about this book

The first part of this book shows you scenes with words and pictures round them. The second part is a dictionary. This is a list of all the words in the first half of the book. It tells you what the words mean, and shows you how to spell them. There is also a picture by the side of each word to help you.

The words in the dictionary are in alphabetical order. It will be easier for you to find the word you are looking for if you can say the letters of the alphabet in the right order, like this:

a b c d e f g h i j k l m n o p q r s t u v w x y z

A B C D E F G H I J K L M N O P Q R S T U V W X Y Z

All the words starting with 'a' are at the beginning of the dictionary. They are followed by all the words starting with 'b', then all the words starting with 'c', and so on.

Suppose you want to look up the word 'ice-cream'. There is a list of the alphabet at the top of each page to help you. The letter you are on will be coloured in. Look for the pages where the letter 'i' is coloured in. Then look down the list for 'ice-cream'.

How to use this dictionary

This Picture Dictionary is divided into two parts, each of which can be used in different ways to suit the age and reading level of a particular child.

The first part of the book consists of thirty scenes familiar to children. Each scene tells a story and contains amusing characters who reappear throughout the book. Children should be encouraged to describe the scene, to guess what is going to happen next, and to match up the margin pictures to those in the main scene. Generally, the margin illustration shows the same view of an object as in the main picture, but some are drawn at a different angle to encourage children to use their visual imagination.

The second part contains, in alphabetical order, dictionary definitions of the 1,000+ words that appear in the first section. Each definition is accompanied by an illustration. Children will usually need guidance to find words listed in alphabetical order. You may like to encourage your child by helping them to look for words, whether to find out what they mean or to see how to spell them.

All the words have been tested with children of the appropriate age.

nose

lips

mouth

tongue

eyes

eyelashes

shoulders→

neck

Your body

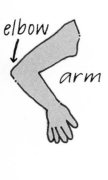
elbow

arm

finger

fingernail

hand

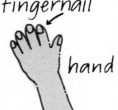
wrist

thumb

palm

eyelids

sole

knee

navel

hip

waist

shoulders

foot

heel→

4

eyebrows

teeth

hair

body

face

ear

jaw

cheek

thigh

leg

back

ankle

chin

calf

toe

head

beard

5

 collar

 sandal

 pocket

 slippers

 t-shirt sweatshirt

 shirt

Your clothes

 anorak

 cuff

ear muffs

hook

hood

laces

trainers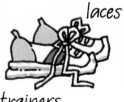

6 dungarees

 braces

 sleeve

 vest

mitten  shoe

 pants

 gloves

hem

tights

cord

pinafore
dress

ribbon

light switch

buttonhole

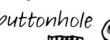

button

cardigan

zip

jeans

scarf

sock

knickers

jumper

plimsolls

dress

skirt

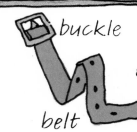

buckle

belt

7

window

In the bedroom

bunk beds

ladder

baseball bat

satchel

computer

flask

pillow

quilt

slippers

leotard

dressing gown

pyjamas

kite

 xylophone

 jigsaw puzzle

 paper

 castle

8

dressing table

mirror

hanger

wardrobe

shelf

drum

lunch box

drawing

bookcase

sheet

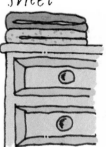
chest of drawers

doll's clothes

train set

crayon

pencil case

pencil

colouring book

doll's house

soap dish

soap

bath

shower curtain

shower

In the bathroom

shower cap

mat

door knob

shampoo

towel rail

10 laundry basket

bathroom scales

floor tile

sponge

toilet seat

toilet paper

fan

cotton wool

cabinet

tooth-paste

tooth-brush

beaker

tap

mirror

flannel

bath towel

toilet

stool

nailbrush

washbasin

11

stool

cup

freezer

washing machine

In the kitchen

fridge

plug

plate

cooker

spoon

light

coffee

bread bin

table

bowl

tiles

sink

tap

draining board

kettle

toaster

oven

clock

frying pan

jug

teapot

cupboard

worktop

drawer

blind

window

door

biscuit tin

13

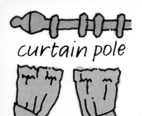
curtain pole

curtain

photograph

candle

candlestick

guitar

rug

comic

mantlepiece

windowsill

In the living room

painting

aerial

magazine

armchair

television

fireguard

fire

video

radio

radiator

telephone

coffee table

vase

loudspeaker

record player

tape recorder

compact disc player

remote control

rocking chair

lamp shade

settee

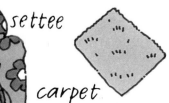
carpet

newspaper

15

bar

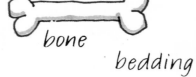
bone

Pets

bedding

sawdust

beak

budgerigar

hamster
house

hamster

weed

wire netting

16 food bowl

tail
puppy

nostril

wheel

water
bottle

tube

dog food

rabbit

guinea pig

hutch

cage

gerbil

nesting box

fur

kitten

tortoise

stand

wings

parrot

claw

paw

17

cheese

spice

butter

eggs

margarine

mince

spaghetti

oil

salt

pepper

Food

pickle

soup

ketchup

grape

pear

chips

hamburger

sugar

fork

knife

jam

honey

crisps

tomato

beetroot

cucumber

cress

orange

garlic

banana

apple

mushroom

potato

cauliflower

plum

onion

pea

cereal

vinegar

squash

juice

rice

bread

19

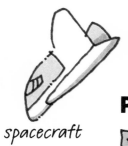
spacecraft

toy farm

roller skates

parachute

glove puppet

Play

skateboard

cowboy outfit

skipping rope

football

Noah's ark

20

dice
beaker
counter

board game
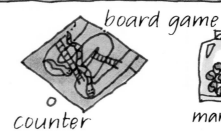

marbles

yo-yo

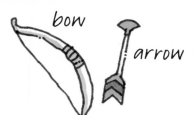
bow

arrow

blackboard

chalk

Lego

target

Plasticine

doll's house

doll

patient

bandage

stethoscope

doctor's bag

doctor's outfit

nurse's outfit

fort

back door

window box

hose

tricycle

step

cat flap

flower bed

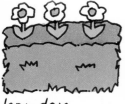
border

crumb

bird table

peanut

coconut

garden bird

In the garden

shrub

dandelion

wall

broom

fork

boot

weed

family

rock garden

waterfall

waterlily

wild garden

tree stump

shed

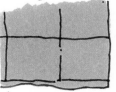
daisy

lawnmower

rake

trowel

spade

flower pot

terrace

23

centipede

caterpillar

hedgehog

newt

Minibeasts

rat

bat

stag beetle

ant

woodlouse

shell

snail

slug

earwig

fly

cocoon

bee

24

mosquito

wasp

butterfly

spider's web

spider

moth

ladybird

worm

beetle

mouse

 flea

grasshopper

tadpole

frog spawn

frog

25

fossil

gerbil

leaf

nature table

map

At school

computer

lunch box

coat

pot

Aa Bb Cc Dd Ee Ff Gg Hh Ii Jj Kk Ll Mm Nn Oo Pp Qq Rr Ss T

toy box

wastepaper bin

clay

paints

paintbrush

reader

26

drawing pin

pinboard

rubber

scissors

teacher

Ww Xx Yy Zz 1 2 3 4 5 6 7 8 9 10

paste brush

paste

ruler

flashcard

library

building block

chart

cardboard model

alphabet

Aa Bb Cc Dd
1 2 3 4

numbers

27

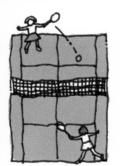
tennis court

tennis ball

cricket bat

cricket ball

stumps

slope

In the park

pram

rattle

baby

pushchair

roundabout

climbing frame

slide

playground

No ball games

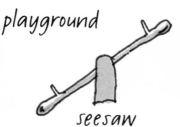
seesaw

sandpit

dog lead

bird

railings

bush

notice
closed

bench

hat

park keeper

litter bin

café
CAFÉ

umbrella

table

chair

island

pond

toy boat

gate

saddle

handlebars

pedal

tyre

bicycle

chain

padlock

29

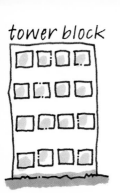
tower block

helmet

tarmac

On the building site

scaffolding

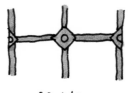

tipper truck

digger

articulated lorry

steam roller

compressor

fire engine

pneumatic drill

loader

dumper truck

wheelbarrow

safety hat

overalls

builder

30

carpenter

bricklayer

concrete mixer

numberplate

H456 ABC

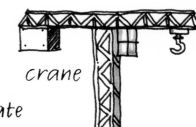
crane

skip

sand

roof

wheel

brick

windscreen

steering wheel

graffiti

bulldozer

cement mixer

poster

low loader

31

ambulance

stretcher

patient

In the town

crossing

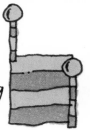

hospital

town hall

lamp post

x-ray

nurse

car

police officer

van

traffic light

pavement

32 wheelchair

petrol station

petrol pump

litter bin

cycle rack

bus driver

bus

telegraph pole

house

garage

shelter

window cleaner

bus stop

car park

bank

cashpoint

traffic warden

shop

toy shop

postwoman

taxi

supermarket

33

 saucepan

shampoo

 soap powder

freezer

price 30P

 vegetable

scales

In the supermarket

handbag

jar

bottle

groceries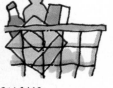

queue

purse

IN

entrance

 receipt

checkout

tissue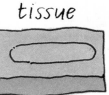

shopping bag

fruit

fish fingers

basket

shelf

packet

medicine

Special Offer!

OUT

tin

exit

arrow

car park

money

wrapping paper

paper bag

plastic bag

card

trolley

field

meadow

In the country

bull

village

hedge

hill

river

Beware
of the
bull

notice

shop

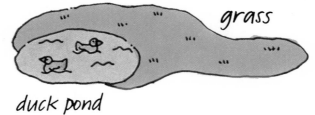
grass

duck pond

cottage

crop

stile

wood

lane

fox

owl

duck

squirrel

weasel

cuckfield

chimney

map

walking stick

signpost

Leeds   Cuckfield

rucksack

37

hay

ditch

horse   foal

pigsty   piglet

pig

On the farm

scarecrow

barn

trough

rabbit

sheepdog

farmer

calf

cow

goose   gosling

cowshed

bull

tractor

trailer

hen

chick

hen house

stable

wall

gate

orchard

ladder

farmyard

sheep

truck

duckpond

duck

duckling

39

propeller

motorboat

helicopter

sailing boat

hot-air balloon

Travelling

cabin

sail

yacht

canoe

bicycle

bridge

tunnel

sign

step

articulated lorry

canal boat

motorbike

oar

40

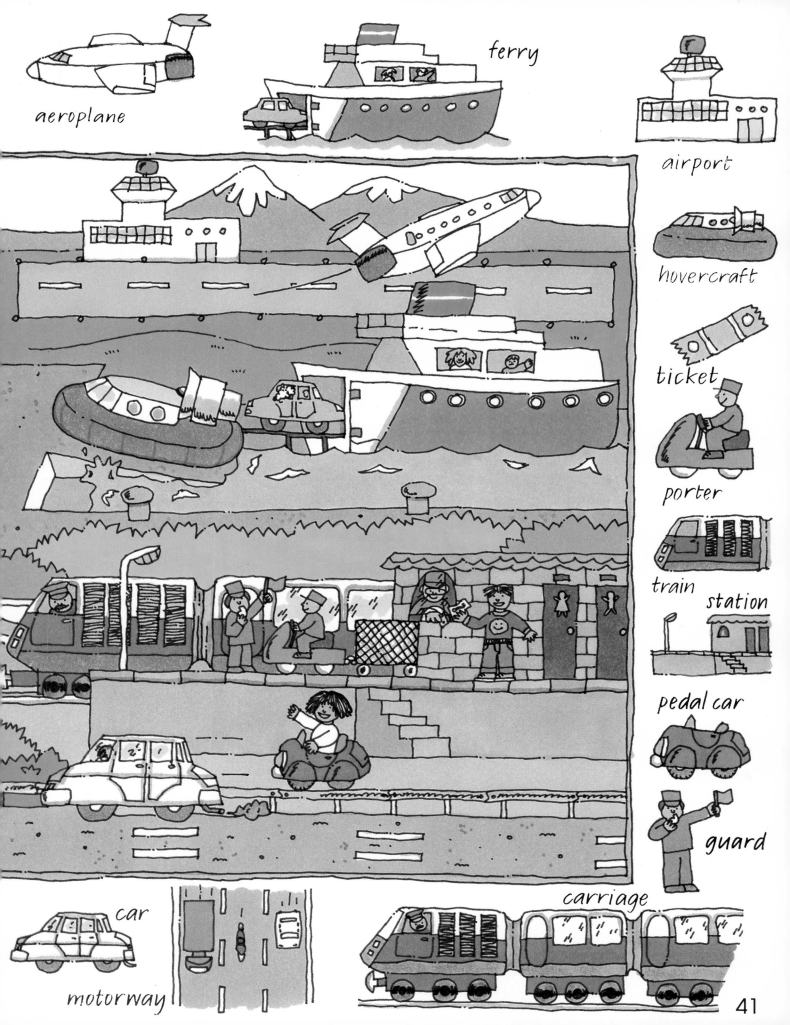

aeroplane

ferry

airport

hovercraft

ticket

porter

train

station

pedal car

guard

carriage

car

motorway

41

hotel

cliff

windbreak

deckchair

groyne

On the beach

suntan lotion

sunglasses

beach towel

bucket

spade

beach ball

picnic basket

snorkel

seaweed

shells

shrimp

shells

armband

goggles

42

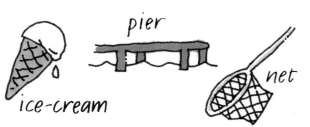
ice-cream

pier

net

pebbles

beach

sea

moat

sandcastle

flag

wave

lighthouse

windsurfer

surfboard

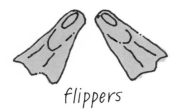
flippers

seagull

motorboat

!lifejacket

sailing boat

 smoke
flame

 awning

 log

 camping gas

 camp fire

 tree trunk

 torch

Camping

 barbecue

 airbed

 washing line

washing

 sleeping bag

 binoculars

kettle

caravan

camp site   tent

water carrier

camp bed

blanket

bacon

frying pan

camera

camp shop

bridge

stream

stove

boulder

bait

fishing line

fishing rod

chocolate

trailer

matches

guy rope

tent peg

mallet

flysheet

tent pole

groundsheet

otter

picnic area

alligator

monkey

ape

hippopotamus

mud

In the safari park

open

goat

stripe

zebra

kangaroo

giraffe

horn

pelican

lizard

wallaby

rhinoceros

46

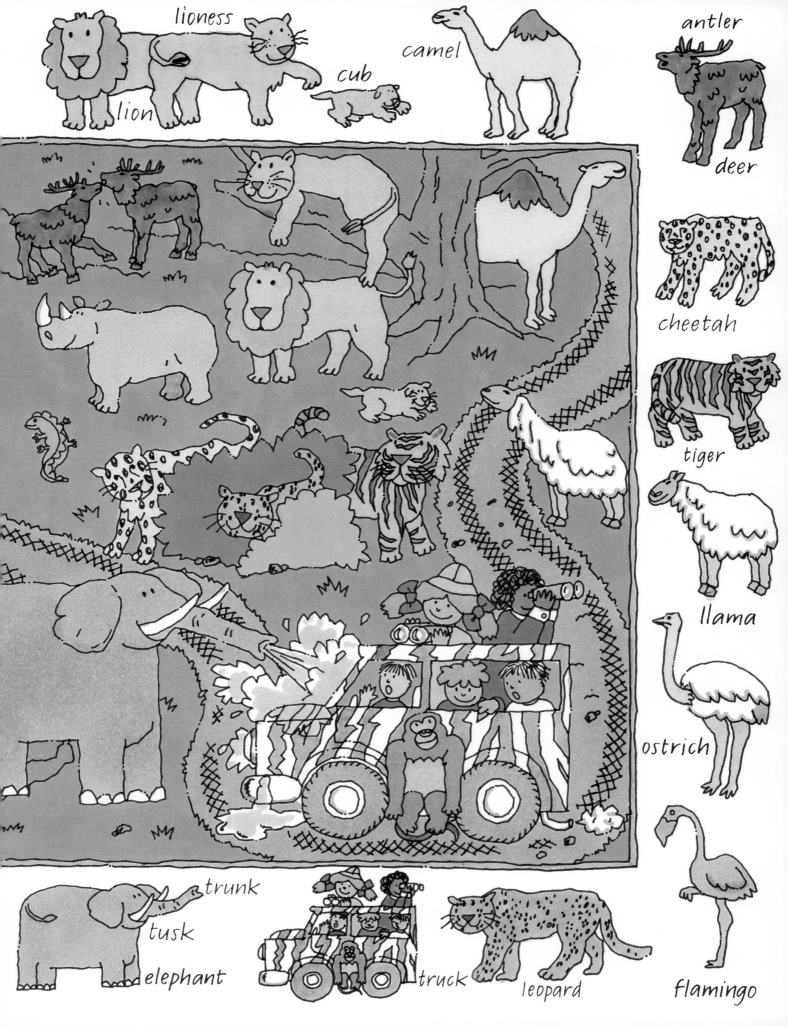

lioness

lion

cub

camel

antler

deer

cheetah

tiger

llama

ostrich

flamingo

trunk

tusk

elephant

truck

leopard

big wheel

raft

ghost train

dodgems

rocket

In the amusement park

headdress

Amerindian

wild west show

parade

paddling pool

miniature railway

pop corn

rifle range

fountain

48

merry-go-round

helter-skelter

cable car

maze

go-kart

tobbogan run

Entrance

Way In

bouncy castle

candy floss

puppet show

snack bar

ice-cream stall

roller coaster

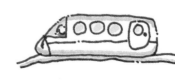
monorail

 balloon

 straw

 bow   magic wand   cloak

Having a party

magician

 parcel

 trifle

 cake

 fairy lights

 paper plate

 hot dog

 paper napkin

50    table

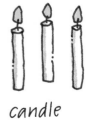 candle

 sausage roll

drink   paper cup

 jelly

cards

party squeaker

paper hat

streamers

ribbon

party dress

cracker

paper chain

handkerchief

paper flower

present

top hat

51

ray

swordfish

seal

diver

turtle

Underwater

walrus

coral

shoal

seahorse

starfish

mast

wreck   treasure

cannon

clam

shrimp

dolphin

aqualung

facemask

whale

jelly fish

wet suit

tentacle

octopus

sucker

sea anemone

cave

torch

oyster

eel

fin

shark

lobster

53

dog run

glider glide

Movement

snake
slither

scuttle
spider

boy girl
walk

horse
trot

gallop

fish
swim

bird

hop

fly

dive

duck

waddle

cat

climb

child

swing

water bird

wade

frog

leap

toad

jump

dragonfly

hover

Sounds

bird — chirp — sing — bird

chicken — cluck — whistle

turkey — gobble

donkey — bray

sheep — bleat

piglet — squeal

pig — grunt

bee — buzz

duck — quack

snake — hiss

56

top

swing

little

big

narrow

wide

long

short

Shapes, colours and opposites

bottom

fat

thin

up

down

pets' corner

sad

happy

soft

hard

old

58

orange

red

yellow

purple

blue

green

pink

grey

white

black

brown

rainbow

sphere

rectangle

star

circle

square

new

short tall

triangle

cube

59

 evergreen tree

 ice

 sledge

 snowman

 snowflake

Seasons

 snowball

 snow

 branch

 nest

 blossom

 lamb

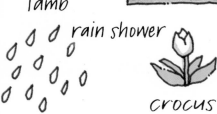 rain shower

 crocus

bud

 daffodil

 primrose

angler

reed

rowing boat

river

riverbank

picnic

sunshine

rose

leaves

apples

squirrel

berries

pears

mist

acorn

oak tree

bonfire

61

gnome

ogre

moon

dragon

goblin

World of stories

audience

sword

plume

helmet
armour

shield

king

queen

treasure

pirate

wizard

cauldron

monster

clown

castle

puppet

giant

fairy

ghost

haunted house

owl

jester

unicorn

prince

princess

witch

broom-stick

elf

toadstool

make-up

enchanted wood

63

Alphabetical Dictionary

Aa

acorn An acorn is the seed of an oak tree.

aerial An aerial helps to give you a better picture on your television set.

aeroplane An aeroplane is a machine that you use for flying.

airbed An airbed is a soft bed used when camping. You blow into a hole to fill it up with air.

airport An airport is the place where people get on or off aeroplanes.

alligator An alligator has sharp teeth and lives in rivers. Alligators can be dangerous.

alphabet An alphabet is a list of all the letters that you can use to make words.

ambulance An ambulance is a special van that takes sick people to hospital.

Amerindian The people who first lived in north and central America are called Amerindians.

amusement park An amusement park is a place with exciting rides, such as roller-coasters and dodgems.

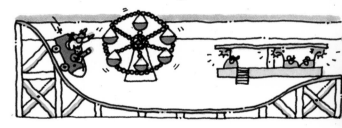

angler An angler is a person who tries to catch fish.

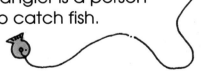

ankle Your ankle is where your foot joins onto your leg.

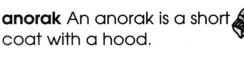

anorak An anorak is a short coat with a hood.

ant An ant has six legs and is very small.

antler An antler is one of the horns which grow on the head of a male deer.

ape An ape is like a big monkey without a tail.

apple An apple is a round fruit. Apples can be red or yellow or green.

aqualung An aqualung and face mask help divers to breathe underwater.

arm Your arm is joined to your body at the shoulder.

armband An armband is full of air. You can wear one on each arm to help you swim.

armchair An armchair is a big, comfortable chair.

armour is special clothing that soldiers used to wear to keep them safe in battle.

arrow
1. An arrow is a long stick. People shoot arrows from bows.
2. Arrows on signs show you which way to go.

articulated lorry An articulated lorry is a truck in two parts. The front part is called a tractor unit. The back part is called a trailer.

audience The audience is the group of people who watch a show.

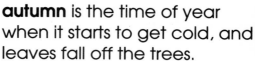

autumn is the time of year when it starts to get cold, and leaves fall off the trees.

awning An awning is a sort of roof made of cloth. You can put an awning on the side of a caravan.

Bb

baby A baby is a small child.

back Your back is the part of your body which is behind you, from your shoulders to the top of your legs.

back door The back door is at the back of a house.

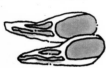

bacon is thin slices of meat from a pig.

bait is food that fish like. Anglers put bait on hooks to catch fish.

balloon A balloon is a very light ball or shape full of air.

banana A banana is a fruit which grows on trees in hot countries.

bandage A bandage is a long, thin piece of white cloth. People wear bandages when they have hurt themselves.

bank A bank is a place where people keep their money.

bar A bar is made of wood or metal. Bars stop animals from getting out of cages.

barbecue A barbecue is a special grill for cooking food in the open air.

bark When dogs bark, they make a loud noise.

barn A barn is a farm building. Barns are used to keep hay and corn dry.

baseball bat A baseball bat is used to hit the ball when you play baseball.

basket A basket is light and has a handle. You carry shopping in a basket.

bat A bat is like a mouse with wings.

bath A bath holds water. You can sit or lie in a bath to wash yourself.

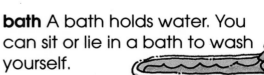

bath towel This is a very big towel. You dry yourself with it.

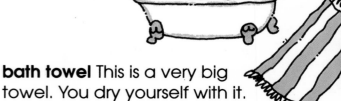

bathroom The bathroom is the place where the bath is. Sometimes there is a shower and a toilet.

beach The beach is at the edge of the sea. Beaches have sand or small stones.

beach ball A beach ball is a big, light ball that floats.

beach towel A beach towel is a big, bright towel. You can use it to lie on, and to dry yourself.

beak A bird's beak is hard. Birds use their beaks for picking up food and twigs.

beaker A beaker is a kind of cup without a handle.

beard A beard is the hair a man can grow on his cheeks and chin.

bedding is cotton wool or wood shavings that small pets use for their nests.

bedroom Your bedroom is the room where you sleep.

bee A bee lives in a beehive where it makes honey.

beetle A beetle can fly, but it keeps its wings covered on the ground.

beetroot Beetroot grows under the ground. It is eaten in salads.

belt You wear a belt around your waist. A belt keeps up your jeans if they are too big.

bench A bench is a long wooden seat.

berry A berry is small and round with a seed inside. A new plant will grow from a seed.

beware means 'be careful'.

bicycle A bicycle is a machine. It has two wheels and two pedals.

big Something or somebody that is big is large in size.

big wheel You can see a big wheel at an amusement park. As the wheel turns, you go up to the top and then down again.

binoculars are for seeing things that are a long way away.

bird A bird has feathers and lays eggs. All birds have two wings, but not all birds can fly.

bird table You can put food on a bird table so birds can eat safely away from cats.

biscuit tin A biscuit tin is for keeping biscuits fresh.

black is a colour. This square is black.

blackboard You can draw on a blackboard with chalk. It is easy to wipe clean.

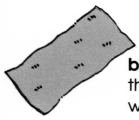

blanket A blanket is like a very thick sheet. It keeps you warm.

bleat When sheep and lambs bleat they go 'baa'.

blind A blind is something that covers a window. You can pull it down, or let it go so that it rolls up.

blossom is the name for the flowers that you see on fruit trees.

blue is a colour. This square is blue.

board game A board game is a game such as snakes and ladders, that you play on a special board.

body Your body is all of you.

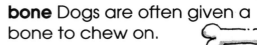

bone Dogs are often given a bone to chew on.

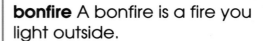

bonfire A bonfire is a fire you light outside.

bookcase A bookcase is a piece of furniture with shelves to put books on.

boot You wear a boot on each foot to keep your feet warm and dry.

border A border is the place around the edge of a garden, where flowers grow.

bottle A bottle is made of glass or plastic. Milk and squash are kept in bottles.

bottom The bottom of something is the lowest part.

boulder A boulder is a big stone.

bouncy castle A bouncy castle is a very big rubber castle filled with air. You can get onto it and jump around and fall over without hurting yourself.

bow
1. A bow is a special knot. You tie ribbons and shoelaces in bows.
2. A bow is also something that can be used to shoot arrows.

bowl A bowl is a deep dish.

box A box is for keeping things, such as jigsaws, tidy. You can usually open and close boxes.

boy A boy is a young man.

braces are made of elastic. They hold your trousers up.

branch A branch grows out from the main part of a tree.

bray When donkeys bray, they go 'hee-haw'.

bray

bread is made from flour. It is baked in an oven.

bread bin Some people keep their bread in a bread bin.

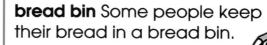

brick A brick is a hard block of baked clay. Bricks are used to make walls.

bricklayer A bricklayer builds walls with bricks which are stuck together with cement.

bridge People use a bridge to cross over something like a river, a road or a railway.

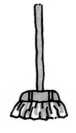

broom You can use a broom to sweep things off the floor or leaves off the garden.

broomstick In stories, witches fly on a broomstick!

brown is a colour. This square is brown.

bucket A bucket is used for carrying things such as water or sand.

buckle You find a buckle on the end of a belt. Buckles keep the two ends of things joined together. Shoes sometimes have buckles too.

bud A flower or leaf grows out of a bud.

budgerigar A budgerigar is a small bird which some people keep as a pet.

builder A builder is someone who works on a building site.

building blocks are for making things like model towers and houses.

bull A bull is a male cow. Bulls are very big, and can be dangerous.

bulldozer A bulldozer is a big tractor. It has a blade on the front to flatten land.

bunk beds are two beds, one on top of the other.

burger A burger is a round, flattened piece of meat, usually eaten in a roll.

bus A bus carries a lot of people. It stops often so that people can get on and off.

bus driver A bus driver is someone whose job is to drive a bus.

bus stop A bus stop is where people get on or off a bus.

bush A bush is like a small tree. It usually has lots of branches.

butter is made from milk and is yellow and creamy. You put butter on bread.

butterfly. A butterfly has four large wings. Many butterflies are very colourful.

button A button is small and helps to keep two sides of your clothes together. Buttons come in many different shapes.

buttonhole A buttonhole is a small hole in your clothes. You push a button through the hole to fasten your clothes.

buzz

buzz is the sound that bees make with their wings.

Cc

cabin A cabin is a small room on a boat.

cabinet A cabinet is a small cupboard. Bathroom cabinets usually have mirrors.

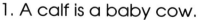

cable car A cable car hangs on thick wires. It can take you up mountains.

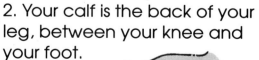

café A café is a place where people eat and drink.

cage A cage is a box or room made with bars. Some people keep small pets in cages.

cake A cake is a sweet food made from flour, eggs and sugar.

calf
1. A calf is a baby cow.
2. Your calf is the back of your leg, between your knee and your foot.

camel A camel lives in the desert. Some camels have one hump, and some have two.

73

camera A camera takes photographs.

camp bed A camp bed is a bed that you can fold up.

camp fire A camp fire is a bonfire that people sit around when they go camping.

camp shop A camp shop is a shop at a camp site.

camp site A camp site is a place where you put a tent or caravan when you are camping.

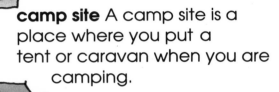

camping If you go camping, you live in a tent or caravan for a short time.

camping gas is a gas that people use for cooking when they are camping.

canal A canal is like a very big ditch. It is filled with water so that boats can travel along it.

canal boat A canal boat is a long boat used in canals.

candle A candle is made from wax. Candles burn to give light.

candlestick A candlestick holds candles so that they do not fall over.

candy floss is a fluffy sweet on a stick. It is usually pink.

cannon A cannon is a big gun.

canoe A canoe is a narrow boat with pointed ends. A canoe only has space for one or two people.

car A car is a machine which people drive along roads.

car park A car park is a place where people leave their cars for a short time.

caravan A caravan is like a small house on wheels. Caravans are pulled along by a car.

card A card has a picture on the front and words inside. You send a card to a friend when you want to say something special, such as 'Happy Birthday'.

cardboard model You can make this sort of model with cardboard, scissors and glue.

cardigan A cardigan is a short jacket, which is often made from wool.

carpenter A carpenter makes things out of wood, such as doors, furniture and window frames.

carpet A carpet is the soft covering on a floor.

carriage A carriage is what people travel in when they go by train.

cashpoint A cashpoint is a machine found outside a bank. It will let you have money even if the bank is closed.

castle A castle is a big stone building with high walls. Children play with toy castles.

cat A cat has soft fur, pointed ears and whiskers. If you stroke a cat, it purrs.

cat flap A cat flap is a little door in a big door. Cats use cat flaps to go in and out of a house.

caterpillar A caterpillar is like a short, fat worm with feet. Caterpillars turn into moths or butterflies.

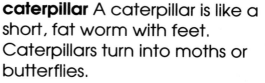

cauldron A witch's cauldron is a very big pot. In stories, witches cook their spells in it.

cauliflower A cauliflower is a vegetable. When it is cut up, each of the pieces looks like a little tree.

cave A cave is a very big hole in a rock.

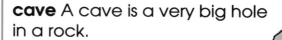

cement mixer A cement mixer is a machine with a part which goes round and round and makes cement.

centipede A centipede is like a very small, thin worm with lots of legs.

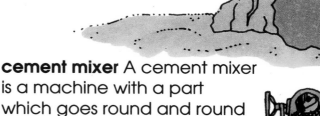

cereal You can eat cereal with milk at breakfast. Some cereals are made of rice, and some are made of corn.

chain A chain is made of pieces of metal joined together.

chair A chair is a seat with a back.

chalk A chalk is a small white stick. You can write on blackboards with chalk.

chart A chart is like a picture with lines and numbers on it.

checkout In a supermarket, the checkout is the place where people pay for things.

cheek Your cheek is part of your face. You have two cheeks either side of your nose.

cheese is a food made from milk. Cheese can be hard or soft and creamy.

cheetah A cheetah is a big cat. Cheetahs can run faster than any other animal.

chest Your chest is the part of your body that goes in and out when you breathe.

chest of drawers A chest of drawers is for keeping things like clothes and toys in.

chick A chick is a baby chicken.

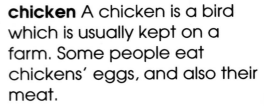

chicken A chicken is a bird which is usually kept on a farm. Some people eat chickens' eggs, and also their meat.

child A child is a young boy or a young girl.

chimney A chimney is the part of a house where the smoke from a fire comes out.

chin Your chin is the part of your face that is underneath your mouth.

chip A chip is a little stick of potato that has been fried.

chirp is a short sound that birds make.

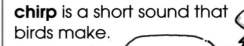

chirp

chocolate is a sweet made from cocoa. You can buy chocolate in bars or in boxes.

circle A circle is a shape. This is a circle.

clam A clam lives in the sea. It has two large shells to protect its soft body.

claw A claw is like a fingernail, but it is very sharp. Dogs and cats have claws.

clay is soft and looks like mud. You can make things out of clay. When it dries, it goes hard.

cliff A cliff is a place on a hill where there is a very steep drop. There are often cliffs by the sea.

climb When cats climb they go up something using their paws and claws.

climbing frame A climbing frame is made for children to play on. You can climb on it and swing from the bars.

cloak A cloak is a kind of coat without any sleeves.

clock A clock has numbers on it so that you can tell the time.

closed If a park or a shop is closed, you cannot go into it.

clothes are the things you wear.

clown A clown is a person who paints his or her face and wears funny clothes. You can see clowns at the circus.

cluck is a sound that chickens make.

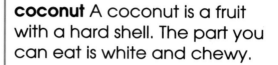
cluck

coat When you go outside you wear a coat to keep you warm and dry.

coconut A coconut is a fruit with a hard shell. The part you can eat is white and chewy.

cocoon A cocoon is a small bag that a caterpillar makes to live in. It stays inside until it grows into a moth or butterfly.

coffee is a powder made from coffee beans. People add hot water to coffee to make a drink.

coffee table A coffee table is a small, low table.
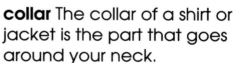
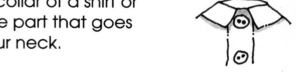

collar The collar of a shirt or jacket is the part that goes around your neck.

colour Red is a colour. There are many colours in a rainbow.

colouring book A colouring book has lots of pictures to colour in.

comic A comic is a thin book with pictures that tell a funny story.

compact disc player This is a machine that plays a small record called a compact disc.

compressor A compressor is an engine that uses air to make pneumatic drills work.

computer A computer is a machine. It helps you work out difficult things. You can play games on a computer.

concrete mixer A concrete mixer has a back part which goes round and round to mix concrete.

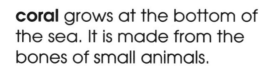

cooker A cooker has electric or gas rings on top, and an oven below.

coral grows at the bottom of the sea. It is made from the bones of small animals.

cord is like strong string.

cottage A cottage is a small house. Cottages are usually in the country.

cotton wool is soft and fluffy. You can use it to clean a sore place, such as a cut.

counter A counter is a small, round, flat piece of plastic. You use counters to play some games.

country When you are in the country, you are away from towns and cities.

cow A cow is a big farm animal that gives milk.

cowboy A cowboy rides a horse and looks after cattle. Cowgirls also do this job.

cowboy outfit Children dress in cowboy outfits when they want to pretend to be cowboys or cowgirls.

cowshed Cows are taken to a cowshed to be milked.

cracker You pull a cracker at parties and it makes a loud bang. Inside a cracker you often find a paper hat.

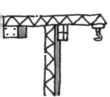

crane A crane lifts and moves heavy things on a building site.

crayon A crayon is a waxy colouring pencil.

cress is a small plant that you eat in sandwiches or salads.

cricket ball A cricket ball is a hard red ball.

cricket bat A cricket bat is a long bat you use to play cricket.

crisp A crisp is a very thin slice of potato that has been fried.

crocus A crocus is a small spring flower. They can be purple, yellow or white.

crop A crop is a food like barley which grows in a field.

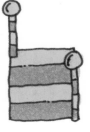

crossing A crossing is a place where you can cross the road safely.

crown A crown is a round hat usually made of gold. Kings and queens wear crowns.

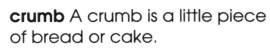

crumb A crumb is a little piece of bread or cake.

cry You cry when you are sad, and tears come out of your eyes.

cry

cub Some baby animals are called cubs. Foxes, bears and lions all have cubs.

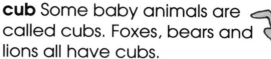

cube A cube is a solid shape. This is a cube.

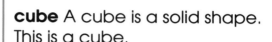

cucumber A cucumber is long and dark green. People slice them and eat them in salads.

cuff The cuff of a shirt is the part at the end of the sleeve. The cuff goes round your wrist.

cup A cup is like a small beaker with a handle. You can drink tea or squash from a cup.

cupboard You can put things in a cupboard. Cupboards usually have shelves, and doors that open and close.

curtain You can pull a curtain to cover a window.

curtain pole You can see a curtain pole above a window. Curtains hang on a curtain pole so they can be opened and closed easily.

cycle rack People leave their bicycles in a cycle rack.

Dd

daffodil A daffodil is a tall yellow flower that grows in spring.

daisy A daisy is a very small flower that often grows in grass.

dandelion A dandelion is a yellow flower. The seeds of dandelions make a fluffy ball.

deckchair A deckchair is a folding seat. You use them in the garden and at the seaside.

deer A deer is smaller than a horse. Deer live in woods and forests. Male deer have antlers on their heads.

dice You throw dice in board games. The dots on the side of the dice tell you how many spaces you can move.

digger A digger is a tractor with a long arm and a scoop at the front. The scoop digs up earth and carries it away.

ditch A ditch is a long, deep dip in the ground.

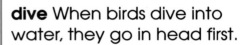

dive When birds dive into water, they go in head first.

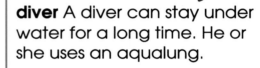

diver A diver can stay under water for a long time. He or she uses an aqualung.

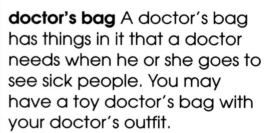

doctor's bag A doctor's bag has things in it that a doctor needs when he or she goes to see sick people. You may have a toy doctor's bag with your doctor's outfit.

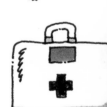

doctor's outfit You put on a doctor's outfit when you are pretending to be a doctor.

dodgem A dodgem is a special car that you can drive at amusement parks.

dog Many people keep a dog as a pet. Some dogs can be trained to do different kinds of work, like sheepdogs.

dog food is food that is specially made for dogs. It can be biscuits, or meat in a tin.

doll A doll is for children to play with. It is like a small person.

doll's clothes look like real people's clothes.

doll's house A doll's house is a toy house. The furniture inside is very small.

dolphin A dolphin lives in the sea, but it is not a fish.

donkey A donkey is rather like a horse, but with longer ears.

door You can open and shut a door. Some doors swing open, and some slide sideways.

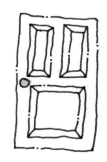

door knob A door knob helps you to open and close a door.

down If you go down on a seesaw, you go towards the bottom.

dragon In stories, a dragon is like a big lizard with wings. Dragons breathe fire.

dragonfly A dragonfly has four long wings and a very long, thin body.

draining board The draining board is next to the sink. It is where you put things you have washed up.

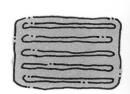

drawer A drawer is like a box to hold things such as clothes and toys.

drawing A drawing is a picture. You do drawings with pencils, crayons, or felt-tip pens.

drawing pin A drawing pin is a short pin with a flat head.

dress A dress is like a skirt and top joined together. Dresses can be long or short.

dressing gown A dressing gown is long and warm. You can put it on over your night clothes.

dressing table People often have a dressing table in their bedroom. It has drawers for clothes.

drink A drink is something you have when you are thirsty. Water, milk, juice and squash are all drinks.

driver A driver is a person who drives a car, a bus, a lorry or a train.

drum You hit a drum with your hand or wooden sticks, to make a loud noise.

duck A duck is a bird that likes the water, so it has webbed feet.

duckling A duckling is a baby duck.

duckpond A duckpond is a small pond where ducks live.

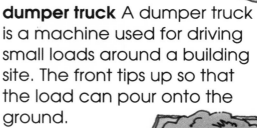

dumper truck A dumper truck is a machine used for driving small loads around a building site. The front tips up so that the load can pour onto the ground.

dungarees are trousers with a high front and straps which go over your shoulders.

Ee

ear You have one ear on each side of your head. When you hear a noise, the sound comes into your ears.

ear muff An ear muff on each ear keeps your ears warm in winter.

earwig An earwig has six legs and two sharp claws to pinch with.

eel An eel is a long, thin fish.

egg An egg has a hard shell and a yolk inside. Many people eat chickens' eggs.

elbow Your elbow is where your arm bends in the middle.

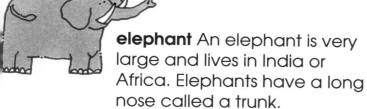

elephant An elephant is very large and lives in India or Africa. Elephants have a long nose called a trunk.

elf In stories, an elf is a small person who does magic things.

enchanted wood In stories, an enchanted wood is a place where strange things happen.

entrance The entrance to a place is the way in.

evergreen tree An evergreen tree is a tree that has green leaves all year round.

exit The exit to a place is the way out.

eye You have two eyes. You use them to see everything around you.

eyebrow Your eyebrow is the line of hair above each eye.

eyelash An eyelash is a little hair that grows on the edge of your eyelid. You have lots of eyelashes on each eyelid.

eyelid When you shut your eyelid, it covers your eye.

Ff

face Your face is where your eyes, your nose and your mouth are.

face mask People wear a face mask so that they can see underwater. Face masks keep the water out of your eyes.

fairy In stories, a fairy is a small person with wings. Fairies can do magic things.

fairy lights are a line of very small lights. People use fairy lights to make their homes pretty at special times of the year.

family A family is a group of people made up of parents and children.

fan A fan is something that spins round. A fan can take away steam or cooking smells.

farm A farm is a place where cows, chickens and sheep live. Farms also grow crops.

farmer A farmer is a person who lives and works on a farm.

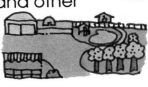

farmyard A farmyard is where the farmer's house and other farm buildings are.

fat If someone or something is fat, they are heavier than they should be.

ferry A ferry is a boat that takes people, cars and lorries across water.

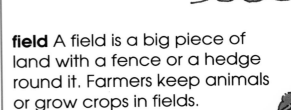

field A field is a big piece of land with a fence or a hedge round it. Farmers keep animals or grow crops in fields.

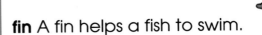

fin A fin helps a fish to swim.

finger You have four fingers and a thumb on each hand.

fingernail A fingernail is the hard, shiny end part of each of your fingers.

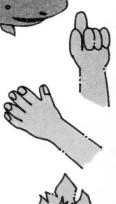

fire A fire keeps you warm. There are wood fires, coal fires, gas fires and electric fires.

fire engine A fire engine is a big lorry with hoses and ladders. The firefighters climb the ladders to save cats and use the hoses to put out fires.

fireguard A fireguard stops children from falling into the fire. Fireguards also stop hot coal from burning the carpet.

fireplace. The fireplace is the place in a room where you can have a fire.

fish live in rivers, lakes and the sea. Fish have fins and a tail to help them swim and they can breathe underwater. Some people eat fish.

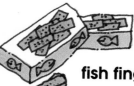

fish fingers are little sticks of fish, covered in breadcrumbs.

fishing line A fishing line is a long piece of string, with a hook on the end.

fishing rod A fishing rod carries the fishing line. Anglers use a fishing rod to catch fish.

flag A flag is a piece of cloth with a pattern on it. Every country has its own flag.

flame You can see a flame coming from a fire that is burning. Flames are very hot.

flamingo A flamingo is a very tall, pink bird with a long neck.

flannel You use a flannel to wash with. Flannels can be like a glove. You put your hand inside and rub your face clean.

flashcard A flashcard has a word or number on it. Teachers use flashcards to help you to learn new things.

flask A flask is a special bottle that keeps drinks hot or cold.

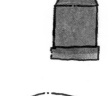

flea A flea is very small and lives in the fur of other animals. Fleas can jump a very long way.

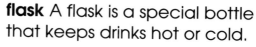

flipper A flipper on each foot can help you swim faster.

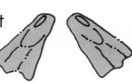

floor tile A floor tile is a square piece of plastic or wood that fits together with other tiles to cover the floor.

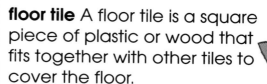

flower bed A flower bed is a place in the garden where flowers grow.

flowerpot You can put earth in a flowerpot and grow plants.

fly
1. A fly is small and black, with two wings.
2. When birds fly, they move through the air using their wings.

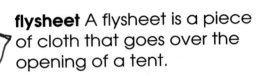

flysheet A flysheet is a piece of cloth that goes over the opening of a tent.

foal A foal is a baby horse.

food is what you eat so that you can live and grow. Animals and plants need food as well.

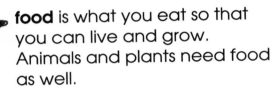

food bowl You put pet food into a food bowl.

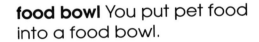

foot You have a foot at the end of each leg. Feet are for standing and walking on.

football A football is a big ball.

fork
1. You use a fork to eat with. Forks have a handle and three or four points.
2. A garden fork is a very large fork for digging.

fort A fort is a very strong building which soldiers used to live in. Children play with model forts.

fossil A fossil is the shape of an animal or plant that died a very long time ago.

fountain A fountain is water that shoots up into the air.

fox A fox lives underground and has a very bushy tail.

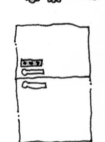

freezer A freezer is like a very cold fridge. Food stays fresh in a freezer for a long time.

fridge A fridge is like a cupboard that is kept cold. Food and drinks are kept in it.

frog A frog has smooth skin and large eyes. Most frogs live near the water, so they have long back legs for swimming.

frog spawn is the name for the eggs laid by frogs. Tadpoles come from the eggs.

fruit There are many different kinds of fruit, such as apples, bananas and grapes. Most fruit is sweet and good for you.

frying pan A frying pan is used to fry food such as sausages and bacon.

fur is the hair that grows on some animals' bodies.

Gg

gallop When horses gallop they run very fast.

garage A garage is where people keep a car.

garden A garden is a place near the house where you can grow things.

garden birds live in the garden and eat worms and berries.

garlic is a plant with a very strong taste.

gate A gate is like a small door. You find gates in gardens.

gerbil A gerbil is a small animal that is often kept as a pet.

ghost A ghost is a spooky person in a story. It is the shadowy shape of someone who died long ago.

ghost train A ghost train is a ride at an amusement park. You go past things such as pretend spiders' webs and monsters.

giant In stories, a giant is a person who is much taller than a house.

giraffe A giraffe is the tallest animal in the world. It has a very long neck.

girl A girl is a young woman.

glide when something glides it moves smoothly.

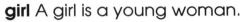

glider A glider is a kind of aeroplane without an engine. It glides through the air like a bird.

glove You wear a glove on each hand to keep them warm.

glove puppet A glove puppet is a toy. It looks like a person or an animal. You make it move by putting your hand inside.

gnome In stories, a gnome is a very small person. Gnomes dress in bright colours.

go-kart A go-kart is a small car for one person. Go-karts have engines and they go quite fast. You only ride them on a go-kart track.

goat A goat has horns and a short tail. People keep goats for their milk and cheese.

gobble is a sound that turkeys make.

goblin In stories, a goblin is an ugly little person. Goblins usually do naughty things.

goggles are glasses that you wear underwater. They do not let the water get in your eyes.

goose A goose is a bird like a duck, but geese have longer necks.

gosling A gosling is a baby goose.

graffiti is any writing or drawing scribbled on outside walls or public toilets.

grape A grape is a small, round fruit. Grapes grow in bunches.

grass is a green plant with spiky leaves. If it is not cut, it grows very long.

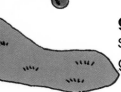

grasshopper A grasshopper is a small animal which can jump a long way. Grasshoppers make a chirping noise.

green is a colour. This square is green.

grey is a colour. This square is grey.

groceries are the things you buy every week, like bread, butter, soap and toilet paper.

groundsheet A groundsheet is a strong sheet that goes on the ground inside a tent.

groyne A groyne is a wall that sticks out into the sea from the beach.

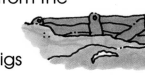

grunt is a sound that pigs make.

guard A guard looks after a train. He travels on the train.

guinea pig A guinea pig is a small animal that is often kept as a pet.

guitar A guitar is a musical instrument. It can have six or twelve strings and makes many different sounds.

guy rope A guy rope is a rope that helps to hold a tent up.

Hh

hair grows on your head and body. People can have dark, blonde or red hair. Older people have grey or white hair.

hamster A hamster is rather like a mouse. Hamsters are often kept as pets.

hamster house A hamster house is a cage that hamsters like to live in.

hand You have a hand at the end of each arm. Each of your hands has four fingers and a thumb.

handbag People keep things like money, tickets and keys in a handbag.

handkerchief A handkerchief is a small piece of thin cloth. Some people blow their noses in handkerchiefs.

handlebars are on the front of a bicycle. When you ride a bicycle, you turn the handlebars the way you want to go.

hanger A hanger is something to hang your clothes up with.

happy When you feel happy, you feel pleased because something nice has happened.

hard You cannot push your fingers into something that is hard. Rocks and stones are hard.

hat You wear a hat to keep your head warm. Special hats are worn for weddings or outings.

haunted house There is sometimes a haunted house in amusement parks. Haunted houses are full of scary things.

hay is dried grass. Some farm animals eat hay.

head Your head is the part of your body above your neck.

headdress A headdress is colourful and often made of feathers or flowers.

hedge A hedge is like a wall made of bushes.

hedgehog A hedgehog has long spikes all over its back. Hedgehogs roll into a ball when they are frightened.

heel Your heel is the back of your foot, under your ankle.

helicopter A helicopter is an aeroplane without wings. It flies by turning its rotors.

helmet A helmet is a hard hat. In the past, knights wore helmets and today firefighters wear helmets too.

helter-skelter A helter-skelter is a long slide that goes round and round a tall tower.

hem The hem of a piece of clothing is the bottom edge which is turned under and sewn.

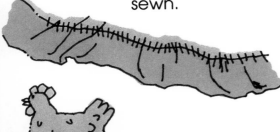

hen A hen is a female chicken. Hens lay eggs.

hen house A hen house is a place where chickens sleep at night.

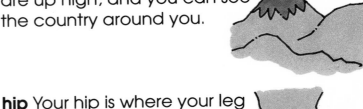

hill If you stand on a hill, you are up high, and you can see the country around you.

hip Your hip is where your leg joins the rest of your body.

hippopotamus A hippopotamus is very big with short legs. Hippopotamuses live in rivers in Africa.

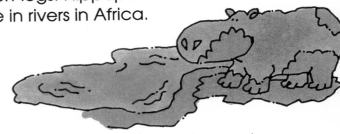

hiss is a sound that snakes make.

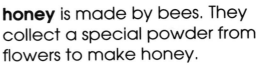

hiss

honey is made by bees. They collect a special powder from flowers to make honey.

hood Some coats have hoods. You can cover your head with a hood when it is cold or raining.

hook
1. A hook is a small, bent piece of metal or plastic. You can hang your dressing gown on a hook on the wall.
2. People use sharp hooks to catch fish.

hop When birds hop, they make a very small jump.

horn Some animals have a horn growing on their heads. Cows, goats, and rhinoceroses have horns.

horse A horse is a big animal. People can ride horses.

hose A hose is a long tube. You can use a hose to water the garden.

hospital A hospital is a place where doctors and nurses look after sick people.

hot-air balloon A hot-air ballon is a very big balloon. It can carry people up into the air.

hot dog A hot dog is a long, thin sausage in a roll.

hotel A hotel is a place where people can pay to stay for a few nights.

house A house is a place where people can live.

hover When dragonflies hover, they stay in the same place in the air.

hovercraft A hovercraft glides over land or water on a big cushion of air.

hum is a sound flies make in the air.

hum

hutch A hutch is a cage for animals such as rabbits and guinea pigs.

 Ii

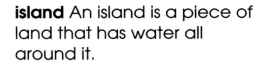 Jj

ice is water that has frozen.

ice-cream is sweet and cold. Ice-cream melts very quickly.

ice-cream stall An ice-cream stall is a very small shop, where you can buy ice-creams.

island An island is a piece of land that has water all around it.

jam is made of fruit and sugar. It is rather sticky. You can spread jam on bread.

jar A jar is a short, fat bottle. Jam and honey are sold in jars.

jaw Your jaw is the bone at the bottom of your face. When you talk your jaw moves up and down.

jeans are trousers made from a thick cotton material.

jelly is a food. Jelly tastes of fruit and is brightly coloured. Jellies wobble when you shake them.

jellyfish A jellyfish looks like a white jelly. Jellyfish swim in the sea. Some jellyfish can sting.

jester In stories, a jester is a person who tells jokes to a king or queen. Jesters wear brightly coloured clothes.

jigsaw puzzle A jigsaw puzzle is a picture cut into lots of pieces. If you put the pieces back together you can make the picture again.

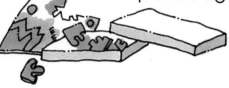

jug A jug has a handle at the back, and a spout at the front. You can pour milk or juice from a jug.

juice comes from fruit such as oranges or lemons. The fruit is squeezed to get the juice. You can drink fruit juice.

jump When people or animals jump, they push themselves up off the ground, and stay in the air for a short time.

jumper You wear a jumper to keep you warm. Jumpers go on the top part of your body.

Kk

kangaroo A kangaroo is an Australian animal with long back legs. Mother kangaroos carry their babies in pouches.

ketchup is another name for tomato sauce.

kettle A kettle is something people use to boil water.

king The king is a man who rules a country.

kitchen The kitchen is the room in a house where the cooking is done.

kite A kite is a toy that you fly in the air.

kitten A kitten is a baby cat.

knee Your knee is where your leg bends.

knickers are girls' pants.

knife A knife is sharp. You cut your food into smaller pieces with a knife.

knight In stories, a knight is a man who wears armour.

LI

lace Shoes often have laces. When you tie up laces, you make your shoes fit better.

ladder When people want to climb up a wall or a tree, they use a ladder. Ladders have steps, called rungs.

ladybird A ladybird is a small beetle. Ladybirds are red, with black spots.

lake A lake is a lot of water with land all around it.

lamb A lamb is a baby sheep.

lamp A lamp is something that gives light.

lamp-post A lamp-post is a very tall light. It lights up the street at night.

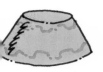

lampshade A lampshade is something that goes on a lamp, to keep the light out of your eyes.

lane A lane is a small road in the country.

lasso A lasso is a long rope with a loop on one end. Cowboys catch cows by throwing a lasso over their heads.

laugh People laugh when something seems funny to them.

laugh

laundry basket A laundry basket is the place where you put clothes that need washing.

lawn The lawn is the part of a garden that is covered by grass.

lawnmower A lawnmower is for cutting grass.

lead People take their dog for a walk on a lead, so that it cannot run away.

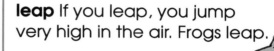

leaf A leaf is the small, flat part of a plant. Most plants have green leaves.

leap If you leap, you jump very high in the air. Frogs leap.

leg A leg is used for walking. People and birds have two legs. Most animals have four legs.

Lego is the name of a toy. You can make things like houses with Lego bricks.

leopard A leopard is a big cat. Leopards have big black spots.

leotard A leotard is like a stretchy swimsuit. Leotards are worn for dancing and gymnastics.

95

library A library is a place where there are lots of books. You can usually borrow books from a library.

lifejacket. A lifejacket is something that you put on when you go out in a boat. The lifejacket will help keep your head above the water if you fall in.

light In a room, a light usually hangs from the ceiling.

light switch You use a light switch to turn a light on or off.

lighthouse A lighthouse is a tall tower by the sea, with a big light at the top. At night, sailors on ships use lighthouses to guide them.

lion A lion is a big cat with golden fur. Male lions have a lot of hair round their neck and shoulders.

lioness A lioness is a female lion.

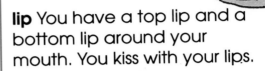

lip You have a top lip and a bottom lip around your mouth. You kiss with your lips.

litter bin A litter bin is for rubbish.

little People or things that are little are smaller than others.

living room The living room is where people sit and read, or watch television.

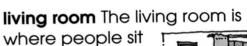

lizard A lizard is long and thin with a long tail.

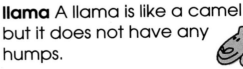

llama A llama is like a camel but it does not have any humps.

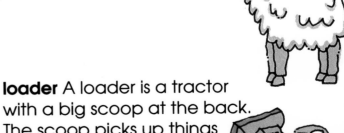

loader A loader is a tractor with a big scoop at the back. The scoop picks up things such as sand and dumps them into a lorry to be taken away.

lobster A lobster lives underwater. It has eight legs and two big claws.

log A log is a piece of wood that has been cut from the branch or trunk of a tree.

long If something is long, the two ends are far apart.

loudspeaker The sounds from a compact disc player or record player come out of a loudspeaker.

low loader A low loader is a lorry with a very low trailer so that things such as bulldozers can be driven onto it.

lunch box A lunch box is for putting your sandwiches and fruit in when you take them to school.

Mm

magazine A magazine is a thin book with a paper cover.

magic wand A magic wand is a short stick. Magicians and fairies use magic wands when they want something magic to happen.

magician A magician is a person who does tricks with things like handkerchiefs and cards. Magicians often do their tricks at parties.

make-up is the powder and lipstick that people put on their faces. Clowns wear make-up to look funny.

mallet A mallet is a hammer made of wood.

mantelpiece A mantelpiece is a shelf above a fireplace.

map A map is a drawing of things like roads and rivers. People use maps to find their way from one place to another.

marble A marble is a little glass ball with colours inside. You can play many games with marbles.

margarine tastes like butter, but is made from animal and vegetable oils.

mast On a sailing boat, the mast holds the sail up.

mat A mat is a small piece of carpet or plastic that you wipe your feet on. People often have mats next to the bath, and inside the back door.

match A match is a small, thin stick of wood. People use matches to light fires. Matches are kept in a box.

maze A maze is a place that you can walk into. It has high hedges and lots of paths. It is easy to get lost in a maze.

meadow A meadow is a field with grass and wild flowers growing in it.

medicine People sometimes take medicine when they are ill.

merry-go-round Some amusement parks have a merry-go-round. You sit in a seat that looks like an animal or a car, and go round and round. In parks, a small merry-go-round with no seats is called a roundabout.

mew is a sound that cats make.

mew

mince is meat which has been cut into very small pieces.

miniature railway A miniature railway has a small train with carriages that a few people can sit in. Amusement parks often have miniature railways so that you can ride all around the park.

minibeast A minibeast is a small animal or insect.

mirror A mirror is made of glass. If you look in a mirror, you can see yourself.

mist is like a thin grey cloud that floats near the ground or just above the sea.

mitten A mitten is a kind of glove. When you put a mitten on, your thumb goes in one part, and your four fingers go into another part.

moat A moat is a wide ditch filled with water. Sandcastles often have a moat around them.

money is something people use to buy things with.

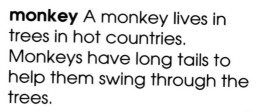

monkey A monkey lives in trees in hot countries. Monkeys have long tails to help them swing through the trees.

monorail A monorail is a kind of train. It runs along a single track high up in the air.

monster In stories, a monster is usually very ugly and frightening.

moo is a sound that cows make.

moo

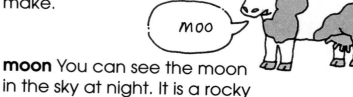

moon You can see the moon in the sky at night. It is a rocky ball that goes around the earth. Sometimes you can only see half of the moon.

mosquito A mosquito is a small fly that bites people and some animals.

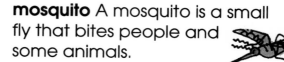

moth A moth is like a butterfly, but it usually flies at night.

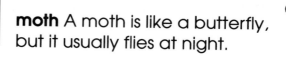

motor boat A motor boat has an engine and can go very fast.

motorbike A motorbike has two wheels like a bicycle, but it has an engine and can go very fast.

motorway A motorway is a big road with room for several lines of cars.

mouse A mouse is a small, furry animal with a thin tail.

moustache A moustache is the hair that men can grow above their lips.

mouth Your tongue and your teeth are in your mouth.

movement When something moves it goes from one place to another. This is called movement.

mud is wet earth.

mushroom A mushroom is a short plant with a white cap like an umbrella. Some mushrooms are good to eat.

Nn

nailbrush A nailbrush is a small brush. You can clean your nails with it.

narrow Something that is narrow is long and thin. It is hard to get through a narrow gap.

nature table In a classroom, a nature table has interesting things on it, like fossils, shells and leaves.

navel Your navel is the small dip in the middle of your tummy.

neck Your head is on your neck.

neigh

neigh is a sound that horses make.

nest A nest is a bird's house. It is made out of twigs from the garden or fields.

nesting box A nesting box is a small box that some people put high up in their garden so that a bird can make a home inside.

net A net is for catching small fish or shrimps.

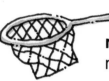

new Things that are new have not been used before.

newspaper You read a newspaper to find out what has happened.

newt A newt is a small animal. It can live in water or on land.

Noah's ark A Noah's ark is a toy boat full of animals. It has two of each kind of animal.

nose Your nose is the part of your face that sticks out. You can smell things with your nose.

nostril A nostril is one of the holes in the nose.

notice A notice tells you about important things.

numberplate A numberplate shows different numbers and letters. Every car, motorbike and lorry has a numberplate at the front and back.

numbers You use numbers to count.

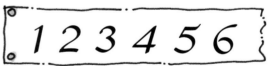

nurse A nurse is a person who looks after sick people.

nurse's outfit You can put on a nurse's outfit when you are pretending to be a nurse.

Oo

oak tree An oak tree is very big, with a thick trunk. Acorns grow on oak trees.

oar An oar is a wooden paddle. People use oars for rowing small boats.

octopus An octopus lives in the sea. It has eight long arms, called tentacles.

ogre In stories, an ogre is a cruel giant.

oil is a thick, clean liquid made from plants. We use oil for cooking.

old Things that are old were made a long time ago.

onion An onion grows under the ground. Onions have a strong taste.

open If a gate is open, you can go through it. If a box is open, you can look into it.

opposites Opposites are pairs of words that often go together, such as tall and short, and fat and thin.

orange
1. Orange is a colour. This square is orange.
2. An orange is a fruit that grows on trees in hot countries.

orchard An orchard is a place where a lot of fruit trees grow.

ostrich An ostrich is a very big bird. Ostriches can run fast, but they cannot fly.

otter An otter lives near water, and swims very well.

oven An oven is part of a cooker. People bake cakes in an oven.

overalls are the thick, strong dungarees that builders wear. They stop their clothes getting dirty and torn.

owl An owl is a bird with large eyes and a flat face. You see owls mostly at night.

oyster An oyster lives in the sea. It has two shells that are joined on one side.

Pp

packet A packet is what crisps, sweets and cereals are sold in.

paddling pool This is a small pool where children can play. The water is not very deep.

padlock A padlock is a kind of lock. It can be used with a chain.

paint You can use paint if you want to make a picture. Paint comes in many different colours.

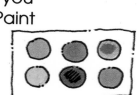

paintbrush You can use a paintbrush when you want to paint a picture.

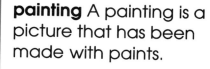

painting A painting is a picture that has been made with paints.

palm The palm of your hand is the flat part in the middle. When you close your hand, your fingers touch your palm.

pants People wear pants under their trousers or under their skirts.

paper Paper is made from trees. You can write and draw on it.

paper bag A paper bag is made of thick paper. When people in shops sell things they sometimes put them into a paper bag.

paper chain A paper chain is made of strips of coloured paper joined into loops.

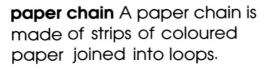

paper cup At parties, people often drink out of a paper cup so that there is less washing up to do.

paper flower A paper flower is made of brightly coloured paper.

paper hat At parties, you often wear a paper hat in the shape of a crown.

paper napkin You can clean your lips and your fingers on a paper napkin.

paper plate At parties, people often eat off a paper plate.

parachute A parachute is like a very big umbrella. If someone jumps out of an aeroplane a parachute will help them to fall slowly.

parade If you watch a parade, you see a lot of people walking or dancing in a group.

parcel A parcel is something that has been wrapped up. Parcels are often sent by post.

park A park is a large open place with a lot of grass where people can walk or play.

park keeper A park keeper is a person who looks after a park.

parrot A parrot is a brightly coloured bird. Parrots live in hot countries.

party A party is a special day when you meet with your friends, have fun, play games and eat lots of food.

party dress A party dress is a special dress that a girl wears to a party.

party squeaker A party squeaker is a whistle with a rolled-up tube on it. When you blow into it, the tube unrolls.

paste You can use paste to stick pieces of paper together.

paste brush A paste brush is a brush for putting paste on paper.

patient A sick person who goes to see a doctor is called a patient.

pavement A pavement is the path beside a street or road. You can walk on a pavement, away from the cars.

paw A paw is an animal's foot. Dogs and cats have paws.

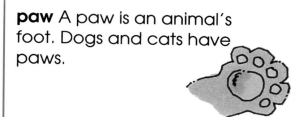

pea A pea is a very small round green vegetable. Peas grow in a cover called a pod.

peanut A peanut grows underground in a shell. There are usually two peanuts in every shell. Birds like eating peanuts.

pear A pear is a juicy fruit.

pebble A pebble is a small round stone.

pedal You push a pedal with your foot to make it move. Bicycles have pedals to make them work.

pedal car A pedal car is a toy car that has pedals. You can sit in the car and make it go along.

peg You can hang your coat and your bag on a peg. It is like a hook.

pelican A pelican is a big sea bird. It has a pocket of loose skin under its long beak.

pencil A pencil is a thin stick used for writing and drawing. You can rub out the lines made by a pencil with a rubber.

pencil case A pencil case can be a box or a bag. You can keep pens and pencils in it.

people Men, women and children are people.

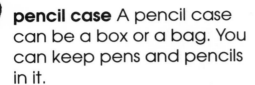

pepper is a hot-tasting powder used on food.

pet A pet is an animal that lives in your home. People often have dogs or cats as pets.

petrol pump You can see a petrol pump at a petrol station. People get petrol for their cars from a petrol pump.

petrol station A petrol station is a place where people go to put petrol in their cars.

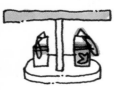

pets' corner A pets' corner is a place where you can get close to some of the animals.

photograph A photograph is a picture that people take with a camera.

pickles are things such as onions and pieces of cauliflower in vinegar. They have a strong flavour.

picnic If you go on a picnic, you take a packed lunch and eat it in the open air.

picnic area A picnic area is a place where there are tables and benches. You can have a picnic there.

picnic basket A picnic basket is a bag to hold the food and drink you need for a picnic.

pier A pier is built out over the sea. You can often walk on a pier.

pig A pig is fat and pink, with short legs. You can see pigs on some farms.

pigeon A pigeon is a fat bird with a small head.

piglet A piglet is a baby pig.

pigsty A pigsty is where pigs are kept.

pillow You put your head on a pillow when you go to sleep.

pinafore dress Girls can wear pinafore dresses over a blouse. Pinafore dresses have no sleeves.

pinboard A pinboard is a large board on the wall. You can pin pictures and notices on a pinboard.

pink is a colour. This square is pink.

pirate In the past, a pirate was a person who robbed other ships of their treasure while they were at sea.

plant If you put a seed in a flowerpot, the seed will grow roots and leaves. It will become a plant.

plastic bag A plastic bag is made of clear or coloured plastic. You can carry shopping in plastic bags.

Plasticine is the name of a kind of coloured clay. It is soft, so you can make things with it.

plate A plate is a flat dish. People usually eat food off plates.

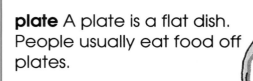

platform The platform is the part of a station where you get on or off a train.

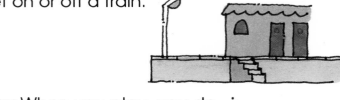

play When you play, you do something you like doing.

playground At school, the playground is the place where you play games with your friends.

plimsoll A plimsoll is a light shoe you wear for sports.

plug In a sink or bath, the plug stops the water from going down the drain.

plum A plum is a small fruit. It has a very hard seed in the middle called a stone.

plume A plume is a long line of brightly coloured feathers. In the past, knights wore a plume in their helmets.

pneumatic drill A pneumatic drill is a very powerful machine with a blade that can dig up roads.

pocket A pocket is for holding small things. Trousers and jackets usually have pockets.

police officer A police officer helps people. He or she can help you if you are lost.

pond A pond is a small lake.

pony A pony is a small horse.

popcorn is a light, crunchy snack. It is either sweet or salty.

porter At a railway station, a porter helps to carry your suitcases and bags.

poster A poster is a large piece of paper with a picture on it.

postman/postwoman A postman or postwoman delivers letters and parcels to your home.

pot A pot is a beaker-shaped holder for a plant.

potato A potato grows under the ground. You can eat potatoes baked or boiled, or fried as chips.

pram A pram is a baby's cot on wheels.

present You give a present when it is a special day, like a birthday.

price The price of something is how much it costs.

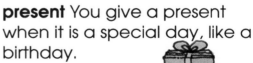

primrose A primrose is a little yellow flower. You can see primroses in the spring.

prince A prince is the son of a king or queen.

princess A princess is the daughter of a king or queen.

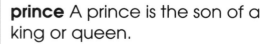

puppet A puppet is a doll or toy animal which you move with strings.

puppet show A puppet show is a story told with glove puppets or puppets on strings.

puppy A puppy is a baby dog.

purple is a colour. This square is purple.

purse People keep things like money and tickets in a purse.

pushchair A pushchair is a small folding chair on wheels. Pushchairs are for babies and young children.

pyjamas are the clothes you wear in bed.

Qq

quack is a sound ducks make.

quack

queen A queen is the woman who rules a country.

queue When people are in a queue, they stand waiting in a line.

quilt A quilt is thick and warm. People often have a quilt on their bed.

Rr

rabbit A rabbit has long ears and a short, fluffy tail.

radiator Many houses have a radiator in each room. Radiators are filled with hot water to keep a house warm.

radio When you listen to a radio, you can hear voices and music that are being sent through the air.

raft A raft is a flat boat with no sides. It is usually made from logs tied together.

railing A railing is a kind of fence made of strong bars.

railway A railway is a track which trains run along.

rain shower A rain shower is rain that does not last very long.

rainbow A rainbow is an arch of many colours in the sky.

rake A rake is for gathering up leaves and cut grass.

rat A rat is like a big mouse.

rattle A rattle makes a noise when you move it around. Babies like rattles.

ray A ray is a big, flat fish with a long, thin tail.

reader A reader is a person who reads words written in a book.

receipt A receipt is a piece of paper. Receipts show that you have paid for something.

record player A record player is a machine for playing records.

rectangle A rectangle is a shape. This is a rectangle.

red is a colour. This square is red.

reed A reed is a long, thin plant. Reeds grow in or near ponds and rivers.

remote control You can use a remote control to turn a television or video on or off, without touching the set.

rhinoceros A rhinoceros is big and heavy. Some rhinoceroses have two horns, and some have one.

ribbon Ribbon is like flat string. It is usually a pretty colour. You sometimes wear ribbons in your hair.

rice is a small white or brown grain. Rice is good to eat.

rifle range In an amusement park, a rifle range is where you can shoot at targets.

river A river is a long strip of fresh water that flows across the land.

riverbank The riverbank is the land at the edge of a river.

rock garden A rock garden is made of rocks with plants growing between them.

rocket In an amusement park, a rocket is a ride. You go high in the air and twist and turn.

rocking chair If you sit in a rocking chair, you can rock yourself backwards and forwards.

roller coaster A roller coaster is a fast ride in an amusement park. Roller coasters are like railways, but they go up and down very steep slopes.

roller skate A roller skate is a shoe with wheels on the bottom. You can move quickly if you wear roller skates.

roof A roof covers a building and keeps it dry and warm.

rose A rose is a flower. Some roses smell very nice.

rotor A helicopter has a rotor. The rotor turns round very fast to keep the helicopter in the air.

roundabout A roundabout is similar to a merry-go-round.

rowing boat A rowing boat is made to carry a few people. You make it move by using oars.

rubber You can use a rubber to get rid of pencil lines.

rucksack A rucksack is a big bag that people sometimes carry on their backs.

rug A rug is a small carpet.

ruler You can use a ruler to measure things, or to draw straight lines.

run When dogs run, they move their legs very fast.

Ss

sad When people are sad, they feel like crying.

saddle A saddle is the seat on a bicycle.

safari park A safari park is a big park with lots of animals. The animals have a lot of space to move about in.

safety hat A safety hat is very hard and protects the head.

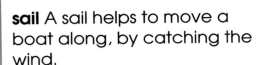

sail A sail helps to move a boat along, by catching the wind.

sailing boat A sailing boat is a boat that uses sails to move through the water.

salt is a white powder with a bitter taste.

sand is made of very small pieces of shell and tiny pebbles. It is used to make concrete.

sandal A sandal is a light, open shoe.

sandcastle On the beach, people often fill buckets with sand to make a sandcastle.

sandpit A sandpit is a place where you can play with sand.

satchel A satchel is a bag for carrying your school things.

saucepan A saucepan is for cooking vegetables and other food.

sausage roll A sausage roll is a piece of sausage meat rolled up in pastry.

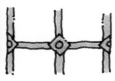
sawdust is made of tiny pieces of wood.

scaffolding looks like a climbing frame. Pipes are joined together against a building so that builders can reach all the way up.

scales are for weighing things.

scarecrow A scarecrow is made to look like a person. Farmers put scarecrows in fields to scare the birds away.

scarf You wear a scarf around your neck when it is cold.

school is a place where you go to learn things.

scissors You use scissors to cut things like paper or cloth.

scuttle When spiders scuttle, they move very quickly.

sea The sea is the salty water that covers about three quarters of the earth.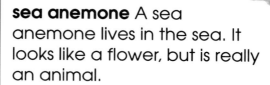

sea anemone A sea anemone lives in the sea. It looks like a flower, but is really an animal.

seagull A seagull is a bird that lives near the sea.

seahorse A seahorse is a very small sea animal.

seal A seal lives on land, but spends a lot of time in the sea.

season A season is a quarter of a year. There are four seasons – spring, summer, autumn and winter.

seaweed is a plant that grows in the sea.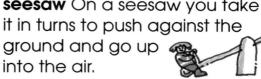

seesaw On a seesaw you take it in turns to push against the ground and go up into the air.

settee A settee is a long, comfortable seat.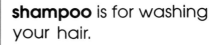

shampoo is for washing your hair.

shape A shape is the outside lines of something. Circles, squares, triangles and rectangles are all shapes.

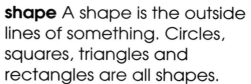

shark A shark is a big, dangerous fish. Sharks have lots of very sharp teeth.

shed A shed is a small wooden hut in the garden.

sheep A sheep is a farm animal. Its wool is used to make clothes.

sheepdog A sheepdog has been trained to make sheep go where the farmer wants them.

sheet A sheet is a thin cover for a bed.

shelf A shelf is long and flat. People put things such as books on shelves.

shell Some animals have a hard shell on the outside to keep them safe. Snails have shells. You find shells on the beach. They are the shells of animals that have died.

shelter A shelter is a place where people can keep out of the rain while waiting for a bus.

shield A shield is a large piece of shaped metal that soldiers used to hold. The shield stopped them from being hit by a sword.

shirt You wear a shirt on the top part of your body. Shirts button up at the front.

shoal A shoal is a group of fish.

shoe You wear a shoe on your foot. Some shoes have laces, and some just slip on.

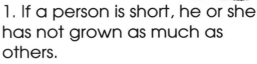

shop A shop is a place where you can buy something.

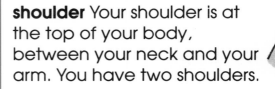

shopping bag A shopping bag is for carrying your shopping.

short
1. If a person is short, he or she has not grown as much as others.
2. If something like a rope is short, it is not very long.

shoulder Your shoulder is at the top of your body, between your neck and your arm. You have two shoulders.

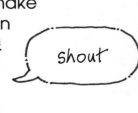

shout is a sound people make to call somebody, or when they are angry.

shout

shower Many people have showers in their houses. Drops of water fall all over you, so that you can wash.

shower cap A shower cap stops you from getting your hair wet in the shower.

shower curtain A shower curtain stops water from splashing out onto the floor.

shrimp A shrimp is a small sea animal.

shrub A shrub is like a small tree with lots of branches.

sign A sign shows people which way to go.

signpost On a small road a signpost points the way to towns.

sing When birds sing, they make nice sounds.

sink A sink is a big basin in the kitchen. You can wash up in a sink.

skateboard A skateboard is a board with small wheels underneath. You can stand on a skateboard and go along quite fast.

skip A skip is a big open metal box for rubbish.

skipping rope A skipping rope is a toy. You use it to skip.

skirt A skirt hangs from the waist. Girls often wear skirts.

sledge You can sit on a sledge and slide down slopes.

sleeping bag When camping, people usually sleep in a sleeping bag. It is warm, but can be rolled up very small when it is not being used.
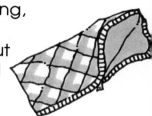

sleeve The sleeve of a shirt or sweater is the part that covers your arm.
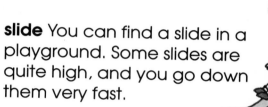

slide You can find a slide in a playground. Some slides are quite high, and you go down them very fast.

slipper A slipper is a soft shoe that you wear in the house.
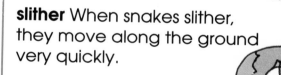

slither When snakes slither, they move along the ground very quickly.
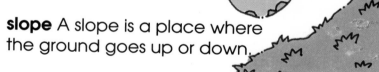

slope A slope is a place where the ground goes up or down.
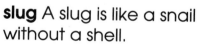

slug A slug is like a snail without a shell.
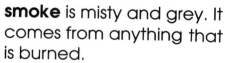

smoke is misty and grey. It comes from anything that is burned.
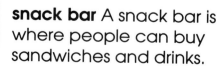

snack bar A snack bar is where people can buy sandwiches and drinks.
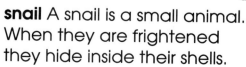

snail A snail is a small animal. When they are frightened they hide inside their shells.

snake A snake is long and thin with no legs. Some are dangerous if they bite you.

sneeze When you sneeze, you go 'Ah-choo!'

Sneeze

snorkel A snorkel is a plastic tube. You can swim underwater and breathe air from above when you use a snorkel.

snow is the name for white flakes of frozen water, which fall from the clouds.

snowball A snowball is a ball of snow. People sometimes throw snowballs at each other for fun.

snowflake A snowflake is a big piece of snow falling from the clouds.

snowman A snowman is a man made out of the snow.

soap is for washing yourself.

soap dish A soap dish is for putting the soap in.

soap powder is for washing clothes.

sock A sock is a soft piece of clothing which covers your foot and ankle.

soft If something is soft, it feels nice when you touch it.

sole The sole of your foot is the underneath part.

sound Anything that you hear is a sound.

soup is a food. People make soup by boiling small pieces of vegetables, meat or fish in water.

spacecraft. A spacecraft is anything that is made to travel in space. Children have model spacecraft.

spade A spade is for digging in the garden.

spaghetti is a food made from flour, eggs and water. It comes in long, thin pieces.

sphere A sphere is a solid shape that is like a ball.

spice A spice is usually a powder with a very strong taste.

spider A spider is small and has eight legs.

spider's web Most spiders spin a spider's web to catch flies to eat. Flies stick to the web.

sponge A sponge is soft and holds a lot of water. Some people use a sponge to wash themselves.

spoon A spoon is specially shaped for eating puddings.

spring is the time of year when it starts to get warmer after winter.

square A square is a shape. This is a square.

squash is a type of drink.

squeak is a sound that mice make.

squeal is a sound that piglets make.

squirrel A squirrel has a long bushy tail and likes to live in trees.

stable A stable is a place where horses live.

stag beetle A stag beetle is a big beetle with horns on its head.

stand A stand is a platform to support something above the ground.

star A star is a shape. This is a star.

starfish A starfish is a star-shaped animal that lives in the sea.

station A station is a place where you can get on or off a train.

steam roller A steam roller has one solid wheel at the front and two solid wheels at the back. The wheels are heavy and flatten the ground.

steering wheel A driver sits behind a steering wheel. When they turn the steering wheel to the right or left, the wheels of the car turn too.

step A step is something that helps you climb up. Some steps are made of stone.

stethoscope A doctor uses a stethoscope to listen to your breathing. You may find a toy stethoscope in your doctor's bag.

stile A stile is made of steps on each side of a fence. You sometimes climb over a stile to get into a field.

stool A stool is a seat with no back.

story A story is about something that has happened. A story can be about something in real life, or something made up.

stove A stove is a small cooker. You often use a stove when camping.

straw A straw is a long, thin tube of paper or plastic. You suck drinks through a straw.

stream A stream is a small river.

streamer A streamer is a very long, thin piece of coloured paper. People often throw streamers at parties.

stretcher A stretcher is for carrying people who have been badly hurt and cannot walk.

stripe A stripe is a line of colour. Tigers have black and orange stripes, and zebras have black and white stripes.

stumps In the game of cricket, the stumps are the wooden sticks that people try to hit with the ball.

sucker A sucker is a small round cup that can be pressed onto things to hold them tightly. The long tentacles of an octopus have suckers on them.

sugar is a very sweet food.

summer is the time of year when it is usually warm and sunny.

sunglasses are dark glasses that people wear so that strong sunlight will not hurt their eyes.

sunshine is the light that comes from the sun when there are no clouds in the way.

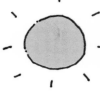

suntan lotion is cream or oil that people put on their skin to stop it getting burned by the sun.

supermarket A supermarket is a big shop that sells lots of different things.

surfboard A surfboard is for riding on the tops of waves in the sea.

sweatshirt A sweatshirt is a light, loose jumper.

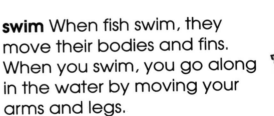

swim When fish swim, they move their bodies and fins. When you swim, you go along in the water by moving your arms and legs.

swing
1. A swing is a seat hanging from two chains.
2. When you swing, you move backwards and forwards.

sword A sword is a long, sharp knife which is sharp on both sides.

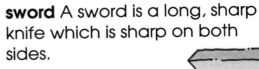

swordfish A swordfish has a long, pointed mouth which looks like a sword.

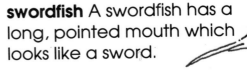

Tt

table A table is something that you can sit round. You can put things on the flat top.

tablecloth A tablecloth is often put over a table when you are going to have a meal.

tadpole A tadpole is a small animal which lives in water and grows into a frog.

tail An animal's tail is on the end of its body. Animals can move their tails.

tall If somebody is tall, they have grown taller than other people.

tap A tap is a handle fixed to a pipe. You can turn water on and off with a tap.

tape recorder A tape recorder records sounds which you can listen to later. You can also play tapes on a tape recorder.

target A target is a round board with circles of different colours. You can shoot arrows at a target.

tarmac is the surface on roads that cars drive on. It starts off hot and sticky and has to be rolled flat before it dries.

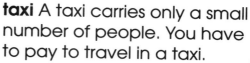

taxi A taxi carries only a small number of people. You have to pay to travel in a taxi.

teacher A teacher helps you to learn new things.

teapot A teapot has a handle and a spout. You make tea in a teapot and pour it through the spout.

teeth Your teeth are white and shiny. You chew food with your teeth.

telegraph pole A telegraph pole holds up telephone wires.

telephone A telephone lets you speak to someone in another place. Everyone has a different telephone number.

television You watch programmes on a television.

tennis ball A tennis ball is a small bouncing ball. When people play tennis, they hit this ball with a racket.

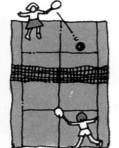

tennis court A tennis court is where people play tennis.

tent A tent is a shelter made of cloth.

tent peg A tent peg helps to hold the ropes that stop a tent from falling down.

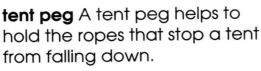

tent pole A tent pole is one of the poles inside a tent that hold it up.

tentacle A tentacle is one of the long arms of an octopus.

terrace A terrace is a flat place covered in paving stones.

thigh Your thigh is the thick part of your leg above the knee.

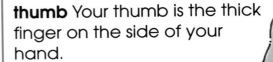

thin If a person or an animal is thin they are lighter than they should be.

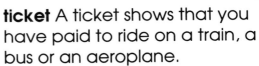

thumb Your thumb is the thick finger on the side of your hand.

ticket A ticket shows that you have paid to ride on a train, a bus or an aeroplane.

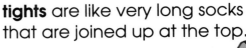

tiger A tiger is a big cat. Tigers have orange and black stripes.

tights are like very long socks that are joined up at the top.

tile A tile is a type of covering for walls. You often see tiles in a kitchen as they are easy to clean.

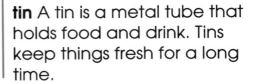

tin A tin is a metal tube that holds food and drink. Tins keep things fresh for a long time.

T

tipper truck A tipper truck has a back part that lifts so that its load can be poured onto the ground.

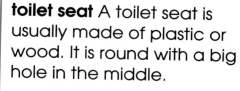

tissue A tissue is a soft piece of paper to blow your nose on.

toad A toad is rather like a frog, but it cannot leap.

toadstool A toadstool looks rather like a mushroom. In stories, small elves often live in toadstools.

toaster A toaster is a machine. You put pieces of bread in it to make toast.

toboggan run In an amusement park, a toboggan run is a ride.

toe A toe is like a finger on the end of your foot. You have ten toes. There are five on each foot.

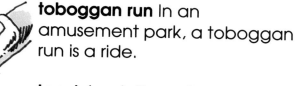

toilet A toilet is a bowl with a seat.

toilet paper is sold in a roll. When you want to use it, you unroll some and tear it off.

toilet seat A toilet seat is usually made of plastic or wood. It is round with a big hole in the middle.

tomato A tomato is a round, red fruit.

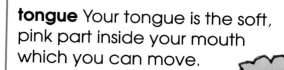

tongue Your tongue is the soft, pink part inside your mouth which you can move.

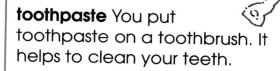

toothbrush A toothbrush is for cleaning your teeth.

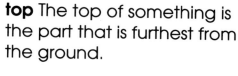

toothpaste You put toothpaste on a toothbrush. It helps to clean your teeth.

top The top of something is the part that is furthest from the ground.

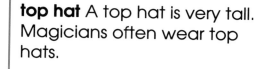

top hat A top hat is very tall. Magicians often wear top hats.

torch A torch is a small electric lamp. You carry it in your hand.

tortoise A tortoise has a thick shell. When it is frightened it pulls its head and legs into the shell.

towel rail You hang towels on a towel rail. Some towel rails are heated.

tower block A tower block is a very tall, narrow building.

town A town is a place where a lot of people live and work.

town hall The town hall is an important building where people can find out things about their town.

toy boat You can play with a toy boat on a pond.

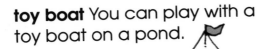

toy box A toy box is for keeping toys in.

toy farm A toy farm has farm animals made of plastic or wood.

toy shop A toy shop sells all kinds of toys.

tractor A tractor is used on a farm. It can lift and pull heavy things.

traffic light A traffic light tells drivers when to stop and when to go.

traffic warden A traffic warden makes sure that people park their cars in the right place.

trailer A trailer is a box without a top, on wheels. A trailer is pulled behind a car. Big lorries also pull trailers.

train A train is made up of carriages pulled by an engine. People travel in trains to get to different places.

train set A train set is a toy train with a small track.

trainer A trainer is a kind of soft, bouncy shoe for running or playing games.

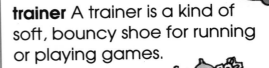

travelling is getting from one place to another.

treasure is a lot of valuable things, like gold and jewels.

tree stump When a tree is cut down, the tree stump is the part that is left in the ground.

tree trunk A tree trunk is the thick part at the bottom of a tree.

triangle A triangle is a shape. This is a triangle.

tricycle A tricycle has three wheels and pedals.

trifle is made of jelly and cake with custard on top.

trolley In a supermarket, a trolley is for putting the shopping in.

trot When horses trot, they go a little faster than when they are walking.

trough Farm animals eat and drink out of a trough.

trowel A trowel is a very small spade.

truck A truck is a small lorry with an open space at the back. Trucks are for carrying things like coal and wood.

trunk An elephant's trunk is its long nose.

t-shirt A t-shirt is a short-sleeved shirt with no buttons or collar.
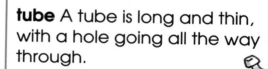

tube A tube is long and thin, with a hole going all the way through.
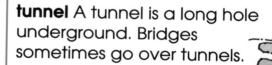

tunnel A tunnel is a long hole underground. Bridges sometimes go over tunnels.
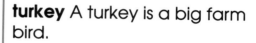

turkey A turkey is a big farm bird.
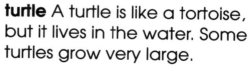

turtle A turtle is like a tortoise, but it lives in the water. Some turtles grow very large.

tusk A tusk is a very long tooth. Elephants have two tusks.
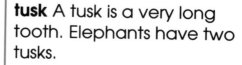

tyre A tyre is a rubber cover for a wheel. Bicycles, cars, vans and lorries have tyres.

Uu

umbrella An umbrella shelters you from the sun or rain.

unicorn In stories, a unicorn is a horse with one long horn.

up If you go up on a seesaw, you go towards the top.

Vv

van A van has a high back and no side windows. Vans make deliveries to shops.

vase A vase is for putting flowers in.

vegetable A vegetable is a plant that is good to eat.

vest A vest is like a t-shirt with no sleeves.

video A video is a machine which plays video tapes on your television.

village A village is a place in the country where only a few people live.

village store The village store is a shop in a village.

vinegar has a sour taste. It is used to make pickles.

Ww

waddle When ducks waddle, they move from side to side as they walk.

wade When birds wade, they walk through water slowly.

waist Your waist is the middle of your body which dips in.

walk When people or animals walk, they move by putting one foot in front of the other.

walking stick A walking stick is a long, thin piece of wood to help you walk along. Old people sometimes use walking sticks.

wall A wall is strong and usually made of bricks. Gardens sometimes have small walls in them.

wallaby A wallaby is like a small kangaroo.

walrus A walrus is fat and lives in the sea. Walruses have tusks.

wardrobe A wardrobe is a big cupboard for clothes.

washbasin A washbasin is a bowl with taps and a drain. You can wash your hands in a washbasin.

washing Clothes that are washed or waiting to be washed are called washing.

washing line You hang wet clothes on a washing line to dry.

washing machine A washing machine is for washing clothes.

wasp A wasp is yellow and black. Wasps can sting you.

wastepaper bin A wastepaper bin is for rubbish such as bits of screwed-up paper.

watch A watch is a small, flat clock. You wear it on your wrist. It tells you the time.

water bird A water bird is a bird that spends a lot of its life in the water.

water bottle A water bottle is a bottle turned upside down for pets such as rabbits and hamsters to drink from.

water carrier People often use a water carrier when they go camping.

waterfall You can see a waterfall where a river runs down a steep hillside. Rock gardens sometimes have very small waterfalls.

waterlily A waterlily is a big flower that floats on a lake.

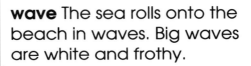

wave The sea rolls onto the beach in waves. Big waves are white and frothy.

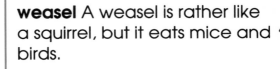

weasel A weasel is rather like a squirrel, but it eats mice and birds.

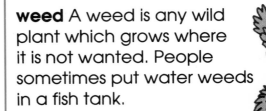

weed A weed is any wild plant which grows where it is not wanted. People sometimes put water weeds in a fish tank.

wet suit A wet suit is a tight rubber garment a diver wears to keep warm.

whale A whale is a huge animal that lives in the sea.

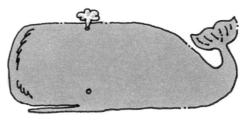

wheel
1. A wheel is a circle. Wheelbarrows, bicycles and cars all have wheels that make them roll along the ground. Most wheels have tyres on them.
2. Small pets sometimes have a play wheel which they run around in.

wheelbarrow A wheelbarrow is a cart for carrying small amounts of sand, cement or bricks around a building site.

wheelchair A wheelchair is a special chair for people who cannot walk very well.

whistle is a sharp noise that people make.

whistle

white is a colour. This square is white.

wide Something that is wide has a large size from side to side.

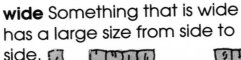

wild garden A wild garden is a garden where wild plants grow.

wild west show In an amusement park, a wild west show is a show with cowboys, cowgirls and horses.

windbreak A windbreak is a large piece of cloth that shelters you from the wind.

window A window is a space in a wall, which usually has glass in it. Houses have windows and cars do too.

window box A window box fits outside under a window. People put flowers in window boxes.

window cleaner A window cleaner cleans windows.

windowsill A windowsill is a shelf at the bottom of a window.

windscreen A windscreen is the front window of a car or lorry.

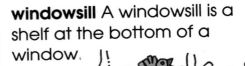

windsurfer A windsurfer is a long board with a sail on it. People windsurf on the sea.

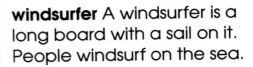

wings are for flying. Birds have wings, and so do bees, butterflies and planes.

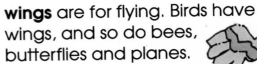

winter is the time of year when it is very cold.

wire netting is used on the front of pets' cages and for fences.

witch In stories, a witch is an old woman who makes magic spells.

wizard In stories, a wizard is an old man who makes magic spells.

wood A wood is a place where there are lots of trees.

woodlouse A woodlouse is very little with lots of tiny legs. Woodlice can curl up into a ball.

worktop A worktop is a flat place in the kitchen where people can get food ready.

world The world is all the land and all the seas on the earth.

worm A worm is long and thin It lives in the ground.

wrapping paper is pretty paper for wrapping presents in.

wreck A wreck is what is left of a ship that has sunk to the bottom of the sea.

wrist Your wrist is between your arm and your hand.

Xx

x-ray An x-ray is a photograph of the inside of your body.

xylophone A xylophone is a musical instrument. Each bar makes a different sound.

Yy

yacht A yacht is a sailing boat.

yellow is a colour. This square is yellow.

yo-yo A yo-yo is a toy. You can catch it in your hand and make it go up and down on a piece of string.

Zz

zebra A zebra looks like a pony with black and white stripes.

zip A zip is two rows of hooks that you can do up and undo with a fastener.